The Real

Bonnie & Clyde

America's Most

Infamous Criminal

Double-Act

Roger Harrington

Table of Contents

Introduction

There have been many notorious American criminals. These include figures such as Al Capone, the infamous gangster and bootlegger, and Billy the Kid, the outlaw and thief of the Wild West. However, two of the most famous American criminals of all time are Bonnie Parker and Clyde Barrow, also known as Bonnie and Clyde.

Travelling around the central and southern United States in a series of stolen cars, Bonnie and Clyde were the terror of store-owners and police alike. There are numerous tales about their exploits during the late 1920's and early 1930's, many of which have been embellished over the years.

Bonnie and Clyde were famous for robbing stores at gun point. But they also preferred to drive the store owners many miles away and release them with travel money to get home, rather than shooting them. This clemency and humanity has meant that some people view Bonnie and Clyde as loveable outlaws, rather than evil criminals.

Bonnie and Clyde also demonstrated their notorious criminal reputation and skill when they successfully broke into the most secure prison in Texas, *Eastham Prison*, releasing several prisoners in the process.

The pair were viewed in many ways. Some thought they were Robin Hood heroes for 1930's America. Some thought that Bonnie and Clyde represent the ultimate romantic lovers, who remained loyal to each other throughout every hardship. Other people argue that the criminal fugitives were the archetype of amoral, vicious killers.

When Bonnie and Clyde were shot dead in a gun battle with police in 1934, the intrigue it produced both at the time and subsequently, has sealed their fate as two of the most interesting and notorious criminals of all time.

Bonnie and Clyde quickly became household names, and stories about them frequently featured in local and national newspapers. The press used photographs to depict the pair as being glamorous, gun-loving killers who smoked cigars and posed in front of stolen cars.

However, what is popularly believed about the pair is often not the entire truth. The reality is rather different. It is possible, for example, that Bonnie Parker, the gun-wielding, cold-hearted killer, never actually shot a single person.

Moreover, many tales that the media published about the pair actually depicted crimes which had been committed by some of the other criminals which Bonnie Parker and Clyde Barrow spent time with.

The Barrow gang consisted of an ever-changing group of criminals who worked on different robberies together or simply evaded capture together. These included Clyde's older brother, Buck Barrow, and his wife Blanche, W.D. Jones and Henry Methvin. These characters are also fascinating and provide further insight into the lives and personalities of Bonnie and Clyde themselves.

Since their deaths in 1934, Bonnie and Clyde have continued to feature as prominent characters in American history and in American popular culture. They have featured in numerous stories and films, and have dedicated fans around the world. However, despite the endless exciting tales which are told about them, there is no story

more intriguing than that of the real Bonnie
Parker and Clyde Barrow.

Background

Bonnie and Clyde operated during the late 1920's and early 1930's in the United States of America. Although the pair traveled frequently, they were particularly active in the States of Texas, Oklahoma, Minnesota, and Louisiana. This chapter will explore the world of Bonnie and Clyde, and the other key criminals that they shared it with.

When the First World War ended in 1918, America had lost many of its young men, who had fought bravely on the frontline. However, the United States had not suffered the same levels of damage to its cities, businesses or infrastructure that many of the European countries had. This meant that it took less time for America to get back on its feet after the years of fighting finally came to an end.

Soon, life for most Americans was generally good, and the 1920s, also known as *The Roaring Twenties*, was a period of glamour and success for many American people. Businesses were growing, jobs and food were plentiful, and Hollywood glamour oozed into the lives of most American citizens. There was a general feeling of optimism and a belief that the years of hardship, struggle and war were firmly in the past.

However, despite the apparent affluence and prosperity, the 1920's was still an active decade in American criminal history. This was largely due to the implementation of the *Act of Prohibition*, which came into effect in January 1920 and lasted until December 1933.

Prohibition was an Act passed by the United States Congress which banned the selling, making or transportation of alcoholic drinks throughout the United States of America. This decision was motivated by the *Temperance Movement* and was designed to improve the moral character of the American people.

Interestingly, *Prohibition* was not a ban on people drinking alcohol. However, the rules of *Prohibition* meant that, in practice, most Americans had no choice but to look to the criminal underworld if they wanted to get their hands on a drink. This meant that in cities such as New York or Chicago, criminal gangs quickly began to satisfy the popular demand for a supply of liquor. They smuggled the alcohol into the city and then distributed it through the illegal *Speakeasys,* which were essentially underground bars.

Prohibition, and the resulting black-market trade in alcohol meant that successful alcohol smugglers, also known as bootleggers, were in constant demand during the 1920's and early 1930s. Many would make their fortune from the *Act of Prohibition*.

These criminal bootleggers had the additional reassurance of knowing that they would be largely left alone by law enforcement. This was because they quenched the thirst of many of the most powerful and influential Americans, from film stars to businessmen and politicians.

It was *Prohibition* and drug smuggling that made men like Al Capone and Arnold Rothstein their millions.

The glamorous prosperity of the 1920's ended abruptly with the *Wall Street Crash* of 1929, and the *Great Depression* which followed in its wake. Almost overnight, people's jobs, money and security vanished, and there was widespread panic over access to food and homelessness.

By 1933, almost a quarter of all Americans who wanted to work were unemployed. Especially for people living in States that depended on either farming or industries such as forestry or mining, there were few legitimate paths to escape the resulting hardship and poverty.

It was against this backdrop of poverty after prosperity that the era of the *Public Enemy* began. The phrase was first used in 1930 to describe the notorious gangster Al Capone. Capone worked mostly in the city of Chicago, Illinois, and was a famous bootlegger and head of one of the most powerful criminal gangs in America. He was eventually imprisoned, not for either the murders or alcohol-related crimes that he doubtlessly ordered, but because of alleged tax evasion. Capone would die in prison in 1947.

After Capone, the term *Public Enemy* was soon used to describe many of America's most notorious criminals. Usually, these were people involved in bootlegging, robberies and murders, whose stories then became splashed all over the popular press.

The title of *Public Enemy* was intended to show that the person did not represent "true American values". The aim of this was to demonize the criminal so that they would be shunned, and the public would actively assist in their arrest. With many *Public Enemies* also being fugitives, this public support was very important to both the F.B.I. and the police.

Public Enemies during the 1930s included gangsters such as Bonnie and Clyde, as well as many other criminals engaged in similar activities. Like Bonnie and Clyde, the police and the media also pursued these criminals ruthlessly.

John Dillinger was particularly dangerous to the authorities, not because of his criminal behavior per se, but because he was often depicted in the press as a loveable outlaw. Men like Dillinger were therefore seen as a threat to society because they were glamourizing criminal behavior. Dillinger was shot by F.B.I. agents after watching a crime film called *Manhattan Melodrama* in a Chicago cinema in 1934.

Baby Face Nelson was an infamous bank robber, who murdered anyone who stood in his way, including police and F.B.I. officers. Both his crimes and his fugitive lifestyle led to Nelson being labeled as a *Public Enemy.* Nelson died as the result of a dramatic shoot-out with Federal Officers near Chicago, also in 1934.

Machine Gun Kelly was involved in kidnapping, robbery and bootlegging. Despite his nickname, Kelly was one of the few *Public Enemies* from the 1930s not to be gunned down and killed by police and F.B.I. officers. Instead, he died in prison in 1954.

The concept of a *Public Enemy* is still used by American law enforcement today. It has been mobilized recently during the war on terrorism, with men such as Osama bin Laden being described as *Public Enemy Number One.*

Bonnie and Clyde were operating at a time when criminals were being pursued and gunned down by law enforcement agencies. The police and F.B.I. were keen to use *Public Enemies* as an example of why, despite the poverty of the 1930's, it was important that American citizens resist the lure of a life of crime.

However, the contextual factors of *the Great Depression* and the emergence of *the Public*

Enemy were not the only reasons behind the crimes committed by Bonnie and Clyde.

Bonnie Parker

The beautiful Bonnie Elizabeth Parker was a young Texan girl, who was born on the 1st of October 1910. Her mother, Emma, had three children, and Bonnie was the doted-upon middle child.

Although as a grown woman she was known for her big personality, Bonnie was svelte at four feet eleven inches tall and ninety pounds in weight.

Bonnie's upbringing and family life was not that of a typical *Public Enemy* gangster. Her parents were both hardworking and law abiding. Bonnie's mother, Emma, was a seamstress, whilst her father, Charles, held a steady job as a bricklayer. But following the tragic death of her father when Bonnie was only four years old, Emma Parker and her three young children went to live in Cement

City. This was a district in Dallas, Texas, where Bonnie's grandparents lived.

Bonnie would remain close to her family throughout her life. Her mother was an incredibly important person to Bonnie. Indeed, Bonnie kept in regular contact with her Mother even during her years as a fugitive.

Emma Parker survived her daughter by ten years and spent much of that time trying to spread the truth about who her daughter Bonnie really was.

As a child, Bonnie was very creative. From a young age, she had a love of photography and the movies. This blossomed into a passion for taking photographs, and she would capture many of the images which made her and Clyde infamous in the popular press.

Bonnie was also a keen writer. She kept an open and candid diary about her life and aspirations throughout 1929. This gives an insight into the motivations and events which led to her choosing a life of crime.

Bonnie particularly loved writing poetry. In 1932, Bonnie spent some time in prison, and during this time she wrote *Poetry from Life's Other Side.* These poems, collected in a small notebook, describe women's experiences whilst living a life of crime. The collection includes frank discussions about sex, love, and betrayal by gangsters. In one poem, *The Story of Suicide Sal* Bonnie praises the protagonist's ability, to tell the truth about her life, when the other women in jail all tell lies about their lives.

Another example of Bonnie's writing is the 1934 poem *The Story of Bonnie and Clyde,* where Bonnie rejects the popular image of herself and Clyde.

In this poem, Bonnie describes herself as having a "raw", emotional nature. Certainty Bonnie's love life suggests that she had an intensely romantic nature. However, contrary to the popular image of Bonnie as a hopeless romantic, her poetry from the 1930's suggests that by then she was becoming cynical about love and romance.

Bonnie had met and fallen in love with Roy Thornton whilst she was still a teenager at school. The young couple was married when Bonnie was only fifteen years old, but within just two and a half years, Roy and Bonnie were living separate lives. He blamed their marriage breakdown on Bonnie's close relationship with her mother, Emma, whilst she blamed Roy's criminal and unpredictable behavior.

By the time the couple split in 1929, Roy had begun a five-year prison sentence for armed robbery.

Arguably though, it was Thornton and not Clyde who was the love of Bonnie Parker's life. Certainly, she still wore his wedding ring, even on the day that she died, and the couple famously were never divorced from each other. Bonnie even had a tattoo of Roy's name on her thigh.

Aged just nineteen, and following her split from Thornton, Bonnie returned to her mother, Emma, in Dallas, where she also returned to her low-paid waitressing job. Bonnie Parker would remain there, writing and wishing for her life to change, until she met Clyde Barrow.

Clyde Barrow

Clyde Barrow's early life was one tarnished by hardship, poverty, and crime. Many of these early experiences, alongside the resulting fracases with the law, would affect Clyde for the rest of his life.

Like Bonnie, Clyde was also born in the State of Texas. However, his family was extremely poor. For generations, the Barrow family had barely made a living working in agriculture, and for them, life during the 1920's was still very hard.

Clyde's parents, Henry and Cumie Barrow, had seven children in total. Clyde was one of the youngest, and both he and his siblings, including his brother Buck, would often go cold and hungry. In desperation, the Barrow family left this rural farming community when Clyde was still a child, in the hope of finding a more successful life in the city.

However, the Barrow family ended up living in West Dallas, parts of which at the time were little more than an urban shanty town. For several months the entire family, including the children, were forced to sleep underneath their wagon because they had no hope of paying for any alternative accommodation. Clyde would have suffered even more than the rest of the family, as he became seriously ill with yellow fever, which the family could not afford to treat.

It would take many months of sleeping beneath the wagon and saving before the family's living conditions could be improved slightly, when they bought a small tent.

The Great Depression of 1929 made finding industrial jobs in the city nearly impossible, and so Clyde, who was just twenty years old at this point, would have struggled to escape the poverty of West Dallas life.

Two years earlier, in 1927, Clyde and his brother Buck had already turned to crime. To them, it was a means of supplementing the meager incomes that the brothers earned through their legitimate jobs.

Clyde had tried hard to find an honest career. He wanted to join the United States Navy, even getting a tattoo of "USN" in his enthusiasm. But due to his poor health, possibly because of his childhood malnutrition and poor living conditions, he could not enlist on medical grounds. Depressed but not completely discouraged, Clyde then took several low-paid industrial jobs in Dallas to try to make ends meet.

Many of Clyde and Buck's early crimes were relatively petty, such as stealing food or returning rented cars to their owners after the agreed time. Indeed, it is almost impossible to see how some of these crimes, such as stealing a truck full of turkeys, could have been masterminded by one of America's most notorious criminals.

However, during 1929, Clyde was venturing into more serious criminal activities, including robbing shops and learning skills such as breaking into safes.

But the most important event, which arguably pushed Clyde Barrow into his gangster career and mindset, was the time he spent in *Eastham Prison*.

The Eastham Prison was opened in 1917, thirteen years before Clyde Barrow found himself imprisoned there. It had been a former convict leasing site. These were places where people could hire prisoners to undertake hard physical labor for them for a fee.

The Eastham Prison had a reputation for making inmates work exceptionally hard, often in very dangerous circumstances. Moreover, as one of America's early maximum-security prisons, it housed some of Texas' most feared inmates and ensured that escape was almost impossible.

It was at *Eastham,* aged just twenty-one years old, that Clyde Barrow was both subjected to, and engaged in, extreme and terrifying violence. Fellow inmate Ralph Fults, who befriended Clyde and later committed many crimes with him, was only nineteen years old.

Clyde was repeatedly and violently raped and sexually assaulted, especially by fellow prisoner Ed Crowder. On one occasion, either as an act of self-defense or revenge, Clyde lashed out at Crowder, killing him with a piece of lead piping. Clyde had never killed anyone before, and in the end, another prisoner took the blame for what had happened. This saved Clyde from what could have become either a life sentence or even an execution.

Not only did the prison guards not prevent the appalling rape, but Clyde also suffered at their hands. Allegedly, Clyde watched guards beat inmates to death, and then coolly tell their relatives they died trying to escape.

Clyde also found the extreme, hard labor that he was forced to undertake so unbearable, that he persuaded a friend to severe part of his foot with an axe, in a desperate attempt to make it stop. Clyde never recovered from this self-chosen injury, and always limped as he walked.

Given these harrowing experiences, alongside daily life in one of the toughest prisons in Texas, it is little wonder that when

Clyde Barrow was released on parole in early 1932, he had irrevocably changed. Described by friends and family as having become bitter and snake-like, Clyde nursed a deep hatred for law enforcement and the prison system for the rest of his life. This hatred motivated many of his crimes, notably his involvement in the prisoner escapes from *the Eastham Prison* in 1934.

Clyde did not return to legitimate work, but instead left prison and immediately became a professional, hardened criminal.

How Bonnie and Clyde Met

Clyde Barrow's family always said that he was a different person after his experiences in prison and that his previously carefree and cheerful personality was permanently ruined. If this is true, then Bonnie Parker was fortunate in meeting him just months before his stay at *Eastham Prison.*

Indeed, in a 1934 poem, Bonnie wrote that despite his reputation for now being "heartless", "cold-blooded" and "mean", she remembered "with pride" how Clyde Barrow had been before *Eastham Prison,* when he was an "honest", "clean" and "upright" young man.

Bonnie and Clyde met on the 5th of January 1930, in West Dallas, Texas. There are many tales about how Bonnie Parker and Clyde

Barrow first laid eyes upon each other. Some historians romanticize the meeting, saying that it was a case of love at first sight for the pair. Others claim that Bonnie was immediately besotted with Clyde, whereas he hardly remembered her. What we do know is that this would be one of the most significant moments in the lives of these two young people.

Emma Parker wrote about the meeting years later, in *The True Story of Bonnie and Clyde,* which is her book about the life of her daughter and Clive Barrow. In Emma's account, she describes how Bonnie Parker had been made redundant from her waitressing job and had decided to spend her spare time helping her friend, who was housebound due to a broken arm.

On this January day, the two young women were busy chatting in the kitchen, while Bonnie was preparing hot chocolate at the stove. While they were happily occupied, Clyde dropped by, to see how the invalid was recovering. As far as Emma was concerned, it was pure bad luck that Bonnie and Clyde met.

Other accounts describe how Bonnie had heard about Clyde through her friend, and having heard how handsome he was, decided to visit the house regularly until she had the opportunity to meet him.

Regardless, the pair were soon spending most of their time together. Within weeks, however, their happiness was ruined when Clyde was imprisoned. He started his sentence in a regular Texas jail, but he soon escaped and was consequently sent to *Eastham Prison* in April 1930.

Some reports claim that when Clyde broke out of his first prison, on the 11th of March 1930, the gun which was crucial to his escape had been smuggled to him by Bonnie Parker. Certainly, she made frequent visits to Clyde while he was in prison, and so had both motive and opportunity. If she did smuggle the gun, then Bonnie was already assisting Clyde in his criminal activities just sixty-five days after meeting him.

The Early Crimes

For many people today, Bonnie and Clyde are heroes as well as infamous criminals. In part, this is because of their early crimes, and the ways in which these have been subsequently represented and understood.

The early crimes of Bonnie and Clyde include helping prisoners to escape from *Eastham prison*, and robberies against rich members of society. For many, these crimes symbolized an attack on socially unfair practices. It has been suggested that Bonnie and Clyde were targeting victims that in some ways deserved what happened to them. This has led some to view Bonnie and Clyde as being champions of ordinary American people, or American versions of "Robin Hood".

Clyde Barrow left prison in early 1932 having been both physically and mentally scarred for life by his experiences there. He was determined to exact revenge against the *Eastham Prison* staff and governors, and Texas law enforcement generally. This was why, as soon as he could walk again, Clyde returned to his previous criminal activities.

Clyde knew that he couldn't commit the types of crime he wanted to alone, and he was soon working within a small circle of criminal associates. These included Ralph Fults, a close friend of Clyde's during this period.

From February 1932, Clyde was selecting relatively easy targets for his robberies, such as small stores and petrol stations. It must be remembered that despite having an automatic rifle, he struggled to run because of the injury to his foot.

The stores and garages selected by Clyde were often family run businesses, which couldn't defend themselves against raids by gangsters with guns. Although this fact does not support the view that Clyde was committing crimes out of a sense of wider social justice, the motivations behind these crimes must be remembered. Clyde was collecting cash and firearms to support his great criminal ambition, which was to enact a raid on *the Eastham Prison* and rescue as many inmates as he could.

Alongside Fults, another regular helper in Clyde's robberies was Bonnie Parker. She had started following Clyde upon his release and was quickly becoming an important figure in the group. Her role was usually a supportive one, and she rarely took part in the actual robberies themselves, preferring to remain in the getaway vehicle.

Clyde's gang were not always successful, however. Just a few months into their spree of robberies, in April 1932, both Ralph Fults and Bonnie were arrested during a botched attempt to steal guns from a hardware store in Texas. Bonnie spent fifty-nine days in custody, chiefly writing poetry and talking to the other female inmates.

However, Ralph Fults received several gunshot wounds and a much longer prison sentence because of the incident. This signaled the end of Fults' involvement with Bonnie and Clyde.

Remarkably, after this brush with prison and the law, Bonnie returned to Clyde and continued to commit crimes with him following her release. Her mother begged Bonnie to leave him, but she remained loyal to Clyde until the day they died.

For a while, the Barrow gang enjoyed some popular support. In part, this was because the gang would often kidnap and then release potential witnesses to their crimes, rather than simply shooting them on sight. Because of their nomadic lifestyle, the gang could often commit their robberies without murder or extreme violence. They did not need to kill anyone if they were able to leave the scene of the crime without being apprehended or pursued.

According to some stories, the gang would even give the people they'd kidnapped money, to make sure that they could return home safely. This, alongside the sympathy which many people had for those struggling with poverty, gave the gang a reputation of being loveable outlaws, at least for a short time.

Victims of these types of kidnappings by the gang included Dillard Darby, who had his car stolen by the gang in 1932 from the city of Ruston in Louisiana. Darby would later be asked to make formal identifications of Bonnie and Clyde after they had been killed.

Many increasingly violent crimes would occur, however, and nearly two years would pass by before Clyde could exact his longed-for revenge against both the Texas legal system and *Eastham Prison*. By the time he was ready, Bonnie and Clyde had already become infamous *Public Enemies* as far as the popular press and law enforcement agencies were concerned.

Clyde's raid on *Eastham Prison* took place on Tuesday the 16th of January 1934. The plan was intricate and took several days to complete.

It began on the previous Saturday night, when Floyd Hamilton and Jimmy Mullens, two men working with the Clyde gang, broke into the *Eastham Prison* complex. The men successfully left concealed guns and ammunition, ready for the Tuesday raid, and then left without arousing any suspicions from the guards.

Bonnie and Clyde sat together, watching proceedings from their getaway car. By this stage, both had severe physical disabilities, and especially Bonnie would have struggled to climb through the barbed wire which surrounded *Eastham Prison*.

That Sunday, Floyd Hamilton visited his brother, who was serving a two-hundred and sixty-six-year sentence in *Eastham Prison* for robbery and murder. Floyd no doubt used this opportunity to let Raymond know the final details of the escape plan.

During the Monday, the inmates on the inside collected the concealed weapons and hid them in their cells. These prisoners included Raymond Hamilton and Joe Palmer, who would both eventually be rearrested and executed for their roles in the escape. Two other inmates involved were Hilton Bybee, who was shot whilst on the run in 1937, and Henry Methvin, who would eventually inform on Bonnie and Clyde and thereby cause their deaths.

As Clyde had planned, these four prisoners would be armed when they commenced their hard, physical labor outside the walls of Eastham Prison early on Tuesday morning. The guards, however, were still unaware of what was about to happen. One guard, Crowson, had repeatedly attacked and beaten Palmer and felt supremely powerful over the prison inmates. His confidence would prove fatal.

On the Tuesday morning, the convicts began work outside the prison walls, watched by a small group of armed guards. They were unaware that they were in the sights of Clyde and his guns.

There are many conflicting accounts of what happened next, but shots were quickly fired, and soon there was a stand-off between guards, the four-armed prisoners, and Clyde and his gang. With Crowson bleeding to death and the guards scattered, the gang ran for Bonnie and the getaway car and sped away from the scene.

One additional prisoner, a robber called French, also ran for freedom in the chaos, but he was recaptured after just a few hours.

Clyde's raid on *The Eastham Prison* was enormously significant symbolically. It showed that escape from the secure unit was possible, and suggested that the prison guards were vulnerable. The Texan authorities were furious, especially with the following celebrations amongst large sections of society, and pursued Bonnie and Clyde to exact their brutal revenge.

Committing Murder

Bonnie and Clyde were living through extremely violent times. Gangsters were increasingly using weapons in their robberies, and in response, the police and public were also arming themselves. Indeed, gun battles between law enforcement officers and high-profile criminals were becoming more common than successful arrests, and many of America's *Public Enemies* were shot dead by police.

Regardless of how Bonnie and Clyde may now be celebrated, it is an inescapable fact that their gang was responsible for the deaths of many people, including unarmed bystanders and innocent victims.

Here, Bonnie and Clyde's gang is defined as the individuals who committed crimes with them, although the actual members changed frequently, and there was never a consistent group of people present at all crimes.

However, whilst Bonnie and Clyde took the blame for nearly all the murders, some were committed by other gang members.

The following cases are those which can be confidently attributed to either Bonnie and Clyde, or to individuals working alongside them at the time.

Clyde Barrow had committed his first murder in *Eastham Prison*. As a result of repeatedly being raped and attacked, Clyde had beaten fellow prisoner Ed Crowder to death. Another prisoner took the blame for Crowder's death, and Clyde was never formally charged.

However, Ed Crowder's murder demonstrated that Clyde would kill to defend himself, and this perhaps allowed him to justify some of his later murders as being acts of self-defense.

The first murder which Clyde Barrow was accused of was that of J.N. Bucher, the owner of a small store in the Texas city of Hillsboro. Bucher was shot during a robbery on the 30th of April 1932. However, in this instance, Clyde could not have been responsible. He was still unable to walk, following the severing of half of his foot whilst in *Eastham Prison.* He, therefore, remained in the car as the getaway driver, and never entered the store.

Clyde's experience of being falsely identified as a shooter by Bucher's widow negatively shaped Clyde's view towards his victims. He now had reason to believe that the police and the public would lie to make him suffer.

Clyde Barrow would now commit several murders, usually with the assistance of another gang member.

The first of these was the murder of deputy Sheriff Eugene C. Moore, and the serious injury of Sheriff C.G. Maxwell, on the 5th of August 1932. The police officers had been called to a dance, which was taking place in Oklahoma. It was a warm and pleasant evening, and the dance was taking place outside. A car was parked near the band stand, and in it were two men drinking whiskey. The two officers approached the car.

What Moore and Maxwell did not know, was that the men in the car were Clyde Barrow and Raymond Hamilton, who were on the run following the murder of J.N. Bucher a few months previously.

Wrongly assuming they had been identified, Hamilton and Clyde panicked and opened fire at the two officers before speeding away into the night. Officer Eugene Moore died at the scene, while his colleague Sheriff Maxwell sustained serious gunshot wounds.

To the public, it appeared to be a cold-blooded execution of the police, and this event would be important in establishing Clyde Barrow's reputation as a ruthless murderer.

This reputation for ruthless killing was cemented four months later.

During the Christmas festivities of 1932, the sixteen-year-old W.D. Jones had begged Clyde Barrow to let him join the gang. Clyde, who had known the boy for many years, accepted, but only on the condition that Jones proved his loyalty to both Bonnie and Clyde, and to a life of crime.

Perhaps for these reasons, Clyde took Jones with him to steal a car from the Texas city of Temple on Christmas day 1932.

However, whether by accident or by design, the robbery turned into a shooting, and the young car owner, a man called Doyle Johnson, was murdered.

It is not clear if Jones or Clyde fired the fatal shot, or indeed why, but the experience certainly gave the teenager an idea of how violent a life of crime really was. Again, the public were appalled that a young father should lose his life in such a brutal way, and Clyde was vilified in the popular press.

But Jones was not persuaded to abandon Bonnie and Clyde after his experience of killing that Christmas. Instead, he remained with the pair.

Just a few weeks later, on the 6th of January 1933, the gang would have another fatal exchange with the police. In a similar way to events in Oklahoma the previous August, this was another case of Clyde wrongly assuming he had been identified and was about to be arrested.

Sheriff Malcolm Davis was, in fact, waiting to arrest another criminal when Clyde saw him watching their hideout. Again, shots were rapidly fired, and Davis dies of his injuries. Eyewitnesses were clear that it was W.D. Jones who had been responsible for the fatal shots.

The gang was now linked to the murders of five people, and their reputation amongst police officers made Clyde convinced that, in the future, the police would shoot them on sight if given the opportunity. Given that three officers had been killed and one seriously injured by the group, this response can certainly be understood.

Clyde Barrow's older brother Buck, with whom he had committed several petty crimes as a teenager, joined the gang in 1933. Buck brought his wife Blanche, who supported the gang by buying food and providing medical help when they were injured, but who did not take part in the crimes.

The two couples; Bonnie and Clyde and Buck and Blanche, and W.D. Jones, rented a house in a quiet district of Joplin in Missouri. Here, the five gang members gambled, drank and generally had enough of a good time to cause a nuisance to their neighbors. One of these said, in despair, that they frequently heard the noise of gunshots coming from the house, often late into the night.

This led to several complaints to the local police department. In the early 1930's, *Prohibition* in the United States of America meant that although drinking alcohol was legal, the buying, selling, making or moving of alcohol was not allowed.

Given the amount of alcohol that was apparently being consumed, the police thought that a small-scale bootlegging or moonshine operation may be taking place, and so they decided to raid the property on the 13th of April 1933.

When they saw five police officers approaching the house, the two Barrow brothers and Jones thought they were being arrested for the gang's previous murders and began shooting.

This was one of the few occasions that Bonnie Parker was seen firing a gun, although she was clearly shooting to provide the opportunity for the gang to escape, rather than targeting any individuals.

In contrast, the male members of the gang were shooting directly at the police.

Detective McGinnis was killed instantly as a result, and Constable Harryman would die soon afterward because of his injuries. A third officer, Sergeant Kahler, sustained serious shrapnel wounds to his face and chest.

Although the police later claimed to have only fired fourteen rounds, they had managed to cause superficial wounds to the two Barrow brothers and to Jones.

In the chaos of the shooting, the gang managed to escape and drive away from the scene, although many of their belongings were left inside the house. These included photographs, which would later be eagerly published in the newspapers, alongside guns, clothes, food, some of Bonnie's poetry and the wedding certificate of Buck and Blanche Barrow.

Just a few months later, on the 19th of July 1933, the gang were involved in an even more serious raid by police. This was in the immediate aftermath of the June car accident which left Bonnie Parker very seriously injured.

The gang had rented another small property in Missouri, this time a cabin and garage at a tourist court called Red Crown. The hope was that this hideout would be a more comfortable base for Bonnie than sleeping in various stolen cars in the wilderness.

To remain hidden from view, the naïve gang covered the windows of the cabin with newspaper. But this drew attention to the group, as did the gang's use of coins instead of dollar bills to pay for their meals at the nearby diner.

Clyde and Jones were soon recognized when they ventured into town to buy medical supplies, including specialist drugs for Bonnie, and food. The local police were immediately notified.

Police officers in several states, including Texas, Oklahoma, and Arkansas as well as Missouri, had been watching for the gang after they realized that the fugitives would be nursing a severely injured Bonnie Parker. The police knew that Bonnie's injuries and medical needs would bring the gang into the towns, and they would be more vulnerable than usual.

This intelligence meant that the Missouri officers could act extremely quickly on hearing about the sightings of Clyde and Jones. They were sent additional officers and equipment from nearby Kansas City, including firearms and an armored vehicle.

By 11 pm all the necessary police preparations had been made, and a group of armed officers, led by Sheriff Coffey, stormed the Red Crown cabin.

A gun battle soon ensued, with the police's submachine gun on one side, and Clyde Barrow's favorite automatic rifle on the other. Sheer luck meant that a stray bullet clipped the horn of the police car, at which point the police officers all stopped firing, thinking that the gang must be surrendering. Of course, this was not the case, and the five fugitives made the most of the pause in gunfire to speed away to safety.

But unlike when the gang evaded capture by the police the previous April, this time the police had seriously injured several gang members.

Blanche Barrow's eyes were covered in splinters of shattered glass. These injuries caused such severe damage to Blanche's left eye, that she never saw out of it again.

Her husband, Buck Barrow, was even less fortunate. He had received a terrifying gunshot wound to his head. His skull was badly fractured, and his brain was exposed. Although it took several weeks, without proper medical help Buck's condition deteriorated.

The rest of the gang tried to stop the bleeding, feed, and calm Buck, but within days they had accepted that he would probably die. Clyde had even dug a grave for his older brother.

Unsurprisingly, Buck and Blanche were captured by police a few weeks later. The group had been tracked to Iowa, where the gang were hoping to stay undetected for Buck's final days.

During this skirmish, Buck sustained another serious gunshot wound to his back, although in his physical condition he could never have outrun the police officers.

Buck Barrow died soon afterward in a hospital in Iowa due to his extensive injuries.

Another notorious double murder, later called the Grapevine killings, was committed by the gang on April fool's day, 1934, which was also Easter Sunday. Here, two police officers were killed by the gang. They were officers H.D. Murphy and Edward Wheeler.

Again, the killings seem to have been caused by members of the Barrow gang who were panicking that they had been identified and were about to be arrested.

Murphy and Wheeler were highway patrol men. They saw a vehicle on the side of the Dove Road in Texas, and pulled over, assuming that the driver needed help. However, the car contained Bonnie Parker, who was sleeping on the backseat, Clyde

Barrow and Henry Methvin, who had recently joined the group.

On seeing the police, Methvin panicked and started shooting.

A local farmer reported what he saw to the police. He claimed that the gang had repeatedly shot at the officers, and laughed as they died. He also said that Bonnie had left the car and helped to kill the two men. The testimony of this witness became increasingly sensational, and it is now completely discredited. Rather than shooting the officers, it has been accepted that Bonnie Parker only left the car to try and give them medical aid. But the local newspapers in Dallas reported every sordid detail of this man's story, and their extensive negative reports finally swung the tide of popular opinion against the Barrow gang.

Soon, there were offers of rewards for the bodies of the gang members, including that of Bonnie Parker. Whether they were still alive was now irrelevant.

The Barrow gang did commit many murders against innocent victims, and these individuals should be remembered with dignity and respect. In most cases, killings did not occur during the enactment of crimes. Unlike other notorious gangsters who would deliberately shoot any potential eyewitnesses, the Barrow gang often drove hostages away from the crime scenes, demonstrating that they wanted to avoid killing people if possible.

However, when approached by police officers, they opened fire without hesitation, often with tragic consequences.

Press Reports

The America popular press always had a love affair with Bonnie and Clyde. Bonnie herself recognized the intense interest which the public had in the fugitive pair. In a poem which she wrote in 1934, she said that the public would hungrily devour any press reports they could find on Bonnie and Clyde. In her typically humorous way, Bonnie then says this is only because the public wanted "something to read".

However, Bonnie also warns the readers of her poem that "there are lots of untruths" in these reports, and that Bonnie and Clyde were not as "ruthless" as the tales reported in the newspapers suggested.

Ironically though, a significant part of the popular image of Bonnie and Clyde was based on photographs which had been taken by the gang themselves.

During a sudden police raid in Missouri in April 1933, the gang's hideout was abandoned. Bonnie, Clyde, Blanche, Buck, and Jones lost many of their possessions, which were collected by police after the gang had fled. Amongst these objects were several rolls of used photographic film.

Rather than remaining as police evidence, these rolls of film were quickly developed. The resulting photographs soon appeared in a Missouri newspaper called *The Joplin Globe* and from there spread across America, and then across the world.

These images, alongside headlines of the latest exploits of "The Barrow Gang", were crucial in turning Bonnie and Clyde into household names.

Several of the photographs show different gang members pretending to hold each other up with weapons. In one photograph, Bonnie has a large gun aimed at Clyde's stomach, in a pose which is threatening but has been considered erotic.

Another image shows Jones sitting in front of a stolen car, surrounded by various firearms.

The image which has endured, and which was the most shocking at the time, is of Bonnie Parker. She is leaning against another stolen car, with a gun on her hip and a cigar in her mouth. The image looks staged, but at the time the public believed that Bonnie looked this glamorous and dangerous all the time. Such images made it easy for the public to believe that Bonnie and Clyde were the hardened criminals depicted in the newspaper stories.

The photographs which the gang had taken also meant that the public could easily recognize Bonnie and Clyde, which would make their fugitive lifestyles increasingly complicated.

The publication of these gangster photographs was the beginning of a significant attempt by many newspapers to demonize Bonnie Parker, perhaps because the idea of a beautiful, young woman engaging in these kinds of criminal activities was considered especially shocking.

By 1934, the pair featured regularly in the newspapers, alongside cartoons calling for their capture and execution. Stories revealed in the apparent barbarity of the criminal gang, for instance telling how Bonnie had laughed as the gang murdered police officer Murphy in 1934. This significantly influenced public opinion towards the gang, which in turn drove demand for more stories to be published about them.

The 1933 Car Accident

Bonnie and Clyde spent most of their short lives together as fugitives on the run from the authorities. By constantly moving between States, they hoped to evade prison, or a violent death at the hands of the police, for as long as possible.

Bonnie and Clyde were, therefore, completely reliant on the motorcar. This was a bittersweet association though because cars also provided the setting for some of the most serious incidents of the couple's lives.

Cars could easily travel between State lines, meaning that Bonnie and Clyde could escape from the police, who at the time, were not allowed to pursue criminals across the State boundaries. This explains why Bonnie and Clyde committed crimes over such a wide area, and why Clyde spent much of his spare time learning the backroads and hidden tracks around the sites he intended to rob.

Alongside the obvious ease with which people and weapons can be transported by car, in America at the time, the best way to travel incognito was by using cars.

Moreover, cars were becoming so common in the urban areas of Texas, that Bonnie and Clyde could return to see their families regularly without the risk of being noticed. They did not have to run the risks associated with other forms of transport or stay in Dallas, where they would eventually have been recognized.

More cars on the roads also gave the pair ample opportunities to steal and replace their vehicle to further confuse the police.

Their car, like Clyde Barrow's childhood wagon, would also increasingly become the couple's home, as their fame meant that using motels or staying in cities became increasingly dangerous. For a time, the entire gang slept in their getaway vehicles and cooked over campfires in the vast American countryside.

Bonnie Parker was frequently the getaway driver for the gang, and Clyde was also a skilled driver. Both were used to driving across difficult terrain at speed, and until June 1933, neither had any reason to be fearful.

However, this changed following a particularly devastating car accident.

It was the 10th of June, and Bonnie and Clyde were speeding through Texas, trying to reach the border with the State of Oklahoma. Clyde Barrow was driving, and W.D. Jones, who had rejoined the gang just two days before, was a passenger alongside Bonnie.

Suddenly, Clyde swerved the car, causing it to crash down into a ravine. Clyde had been driving towards a local bridge, not realizing that it was closed because of repair work. Too late, he had tried to stop the car but had been unable to do so. The car flipped over, before setting alight. Several onlookers, including local farm workers, ran to the scene as the flames engulfed the vehicle.

Clyde Barrow and W.D. Jones managed to escape relatively unscathed. But neither of the men could get Bonnie Parker out of the vehicle. It took several minutes, and the help of several onlookers, to free Bonnie.

By this time, Bonnie Parker had suffered near fatal injuries. The worst of these were the terrible burns along her right leg, which eye-witnesses said must have been caused by corrosive battery acid. It took over a month before Bonnie was out of danger, during which time she had no access to medical help, and was entirely dependent on Clyde, his sister-in-law Blanche, and Bonnie's own sister Billie.

Bonnie would never walk again and was reduced to either hopping on one leg, or on occasion being carried by the still- limping Clyde. The devastating accident perhaps cemented the pair's belief that they would soon die in a violent way.

The Deaths of Bonnie and Clyde: The Popular Myth

Bonnie and Clyde are almost as famous for their dramatic and sensational deaths, as they are for any of the crimes they committed during their lives. The gangsters were killed during a ferocious gun battle with police, during which hundreds of shots were fired, and Bonnie and Clyde, refusing to abandon each other, died side by side.

Whilst many of America's *Public Enemies* were killed in a similar manner, Bonnie and Clyde's final moments seemed to perfectly capture the spirit of the age of the fugitive gangster, which would become forever romanticized and immortalized in American Popular Culture.

The official version of events, which were quickly reported in the press, are as follows.

Bonnie and Clyde were killed on Wednesday 23rd of May 1934. As Bonnie had ominously predicted, the pair would die violently. But their deaths did not occur during a robbery or a high-speed getaway. Instead, Bonnie and Clyde were caught unawares by a heavily armed group of federal officers, when the pair thought that they were relatively safe.

The day had started in a very ordinary way. Bonnie and Clyde had stolen a Ford V8 car, which was a powerful but relatively common type of automobile. The car belonged to a lady called Ruth Warren, who lived in Kansas, but it's license plates had already been switched with those of an Arkansas vehicle.

Bonnie and Clyde were driving this car along a quiet country road near Bienville, in Louisiana. The road was lined with tall pine trees and bushes on either side. It was around 9.15 am and broad daylight, but the pair were confident that they were not being pursued.

In the past, Bonnie and Clyde had traveled using a plethora of stolen cars. For additional security, these cars would have their license plates switched regularly. This approach, combined with Clyde's knowledge of backroads and shortcuts, had made the pair very hard for the police to track. True, on this particular Wednesday witnesses saw their car traveling down the road at speed, but this would have been due to Clyde's general driving habits, rather than out of any sense of imminent danger.

The couple were neither traveling to nor from a crime scene but were driving through Louisiana on a personal errand. They were aiming for the parent's house of fellow gang member, Henry Methvin.

Bonnie and Clyde had been having a small party at the Black Lake in Louisiana two nights previously, which Henry Methvin and some members of his family had been invited to. At some point during this party, Bonnie and Clyde agreed to leave Methvin and to collect him from his parent's house on the Wednesday morning. This would allow Methvin to go home to visit his friends and family for a couple of days.

Visiting friends and family would seem to be a remarkably dangerous thing to do, especially given the inevitable fact that the police would be watching these family members closely. However, such visits were not unusual in Bonnie and Clyde's criminal group. In fact, the gang frequently visited friends and family members, especially in West Dallas in Texas, where both Clyde Barrow and Bonnie Parker had family. Bonnie for instance famously visited her mother regularly throughout him and Clyde's fugitive years, without being caught by the police.

But what the pair didn't realize was that they were, in fact, being hunted by police and that they were driving into a carefully planned trap.

The orchestrator of the ambush of Bonnie and Clyde was a Texan Sheriff called Francis Hamer.

Hamer was fifty-years-old and was brought out of retirement specifically to head the Bonnie and Clyde police investigation. He had a fearsome reputation for doggedly pursuing what he thought was the right thing to do. Hamer also had no qualms about killing criminals and had shot at least fifty-three such individuals during his career.

Hamer's likely misogyny also meant that he would not shirk from shooting Bonnie Parker. Two years previously, in 1932, Hamer had retired from the Texas Rangers because the state of Texas had elected a female governor.

Sheriff Hamer worked with the cooperation of Lee Simmons, the head of the Texan law enforcement agency, and head of *Eastham Prison*. Clyde Barrow was not only a former inmate of this prison but had intensely embarrassed Simmons when he staged a successful escape on the 16th of January 1934. For Simmons, the hunt for Bonnie and Clyde was intensely personal, which gave Hamer access to significant levels of support.

Less than a month after the prison break, on the 12th of February, Hamer began the painstaking process of tracking Bonnie and Clyde.

According to the official version of events, Hamer would correctly locate the fugitives in just one-hundred days, after years of previous searching had found little more of Bonnie and Clyde than photographs and junk.

Hamer had been carefully recording sightings of Bonnie and Clyde, including where and when they were committing their robberies and murders. Although the pair's lightning raids involved using vehicles that were difficult to trace, Hamer had noticed some patterns which were forming in the gang's behavior.

Soon Hamer knew that part of the criminals' plan was to stay close to the state boundary lines. This was a sensible idea. At the time, there was a law which prevented police officers from chasing people across state lines. In effect, this meant that if Bonnie and Clyde were located, they would only need to beat the police to the nearest boundary line, and they would be free. For both Bonnie and Clyde, who at this point were both skilled getaway drivers, this law was ideal and exploiting it would keep them safe.

But by staying close to the state boundary lines, the gang were becoming predictable. Using the locations of previous crimes, Hamer was soon able to plot the gang's route and where they would probably strike next.

On this evidence, Hamer assembled a group of six officers and headed to Louisiana to intercept Bonnie and Clyde. Because of the location of the potential arrests, two Louisiana officers, Prentiss Morel Oakley and Henderson Jordan, were asked to join the posse. Also in the group were four police officers from Texas. These were Sheriff Hamer himself, Bob Alcorn, "Manny" Gault and Ted Hinton.

Hinton was only twenty-nine years old and was mainly recruited because he had met Clyde Barrow and his family, and would, therefore, be able to confirm Clyde's identity.

Interestingly, in his 1979 post-humous autobiography *Ambush*, Ted Hinton confessed that he also knew Bonnie Parker. Hinton had been raised in Dallas, Texas, just like Bonnie and Clyde had, although he was five years older than Clyde. Hinton had met the young Bonnie several times at Marco's Café, while she was working there as a waitress. He was very attracted to the beautiful and charismatic Bonnie, and he wrote in *Ambush* that this had made the police-shooting in 1934 intensely personal for him.

Based on Hamer's predictions, on the 21st of May, the four Texan members of the police posse had arrived at Shreveport, which is a large city in Louisiana. The police were now in the same state as Bonnie and Clyde and were closing the gap with the fugitives.

On the same day, Hamer received intelligence confirming not only that the police posse were very close to the gang, but also that Bonnie and Clyde were imminently due to travel to Henry Methvin's parent's house. Hamer and the posse now had all the information they needed to organize an ambush.

Hamer acted immediately. He contacted the Louisiana officers Jordan and Oakley and told them what he had learned. The posse of six then immediately traveled to the country road in Louisiana and prepared themselves for a stake out.

The ambush point was ready by nine o'clock that evening. The police were taking no chances, especially given how dangerous Bonnie and Clyde were when cornered.

Many police officers had been killed at the hands of the gang during previous arrest attempts. Therefore, Hamer and his men were heavily armed, with an arsenal including automatic rifles, pistols, and shotguns.

All the six police officers needed to do was sit and wait for Bonnie and Clyde.

The police's patience was rewarded at around 9.15 on Wednesday the 23rd of May when the officers heard a car approaching their position at speed. Hinton positively identified the fugitives in the Ford V8 from his position and signaled to the others that this was Bonnie and Clyde.

The police officers provide differing statements as to what occurred next. In early versions, the police made clear that they had tried to stop Bonnie and Clyde and had encouraged them to surrender peacefully.

However, shots were soon fired.

The police alone fired around one hundred and thirty rounds during the gun battle. Indeed, the sound of the gunfire was so loud that by the time it finally stopped, the police were briefly made deaf.

When the police were confident that the battle was over, they approached the Ford V8. It was clear that both Bonnie Parker and Clyde Barrow were dead.

When the coroner examined the bodies of Bonnie and Clyde, he recorded finding seventeen gunshot wounds on Clyde, and twenty-six on Bonnie. Most of these shots were potentially killer blows, including a significant number to their heads, and one to Bonnie's spine which had nearly severed it.

It has been suggested by subsequent researchers that the injuries suffered by the couple were significantly greater. However, they allege that the coroner, Dr. Wade, was encouraged to only report accurate shots. This would make the police appear calmer and more focused in their shooting.

Alongside the bodies, the police also found large numbers of firearms and various car license plates inside the vehicle.

The car was quickly taken to nearby Arcadia. Here Bonnie and Clyde were formally identified by both family members and by H.D. Darby and Sophia Stone. These two people had been kidnapped by Bonnie and Clyde in April 1933, from Ruston in Louisiana.

Even though Bonnie and Clyde had refused to abandon each other in life, they were separated in death. This was largely on the insistence of Emma Parker, Bonnie's mother. Instead, the pair were buried in separate cemeteries in their home town of Dallas,

Texas. Bonnie was buried alone, while Clyde is buried with his brother "Buck" Marvin.

Whilst the police ambush on the 23rd of May signaled the end of their crimes, it did not signal the end of Bonnie and Clyde. As Clyde's epitaph prophetically reads, they might have been "gone", but Bonnie and Clyde would not be "forgotten".

The Deaths of Bonnie and Clyde: The Reality

Inevitably, given the notoriety of Bonnie and Clyde during their lives, and the dramatic nature of their deaths, there has been an intense public interest in the pair ever since. This has led to many alternative theories about the events which took place on Wednesday 23rd May 1934. These have both exposed some additionally gruesome information and brought into question the official version of events.

In a poem called *The Trail's End* or *The Story of Bonnie and Clyde,* which Bonnie Parker had given to her mother Emma just two weeks earlier, the young criminal had predicted how she would die. Bonnie wrote that both herself and Clyde would be killed together, and she seemed to be expecting to be treated ruthlessly and brutally by the police.

What Bonnie Parker may not have realized was how brutally both she and Clyde Barrow would be treated by the public.

Immediately after the gun battle had taken place, Sheriff Hamer and four of the other officers went to the nearest town to report what had happened, and to arrange for a formal identification of the deceased to take place. Quickly, however, the news of the deaths of Bonnie and Clyde on the Louisiana road had spread, and by the time that Sheriff Hamer and his colleagues returned, a mob was surrounding the Ford V8.

Far from being in control of the situation, police officers Alcorn and Gault were helplessly looking on, as members of the public frantically tried to snatch souvenirs from the scene.

Whilst some wanted shell casings or items from the car, others had more macabre intentions. Officer Hinton said that when they arrived, one man was severing Clyde's finger, whilst another man was removing one of his ears. Pieces of Bonnie's hair and clothing were already missing and were soon being sold to collectors around the world.

Eventually, the police regained some control, but it was clear that they were not prepared for the public's response to their operation.

This was not the only criticism that would be made of the police, or of their version of events.

Another accusation is about the police's version of events leading up to the ambush. The police had claimed that it was chiefly because of Sheriff Hamer's careful research and mapping of Bonnie and Clyde's movements that he located the fugitives. But it is now believed that this is not the whole story.

It is important to remember that following the *Eastham Prison* escape, there were many powerful Texans who wanted the young couple dead. These included powerful men in business and law. This knowledge has led to several alternative explanations as to how Sheriff Hamer managed to successfully find and kill the fugitive pair.

One suggestion is that Lee Simmons was involved in a blackmailing plot to kill Bonnie and Clyde. Simmons oversaw the *Eastham Prison* and was one of the heads of Texan Law enforcement. Simmons had promised to revenge the death of one of his guards, a man called Crowson, and to reestablish the reputation of the Texan law enforcement agencies. He was determined to see Bonnie

Parker and Clive Barrow receive justice, preferably he wanted the pair dead.

This was why Simmons made the decision to recruit Sheriff Hamer, who was retired at the time, to conduct the case. Simmons was impressed because of Hamer's reputation of killing criminals on sight rather than allowing them to escape.

Whereas in the popular press it was the police's methods of tracking and calculation that were celebrated, the truth of how Sherriff Hamer knew that Bonnie and Clyde would be on the Louisiana road is very different and far more mundane.

Simmons and Hamer devised a simple but effective blackmail plot, which required an informant from the criminal gang itself to ensure that the police could find Bonnie and Clyde.

Ironically, the man that was selected to assist Simmons and Hamer to find and kill Bonnie and Clyde, was one of the inmates who Clyde had helped to escape from *Eastham Prison*, Henry Methvin.

Quite simply, Lee Simmons gave Sheriff Hamer the power to give Henry Methvin, a member of the Bonnie and Clyde gang, a free pardon, in exchange for the lives of Bonnie and Clyde. The police could easily blackmail Methvin, knowing that if he refused to do as they wanted, they would simply execute him.

Methvin would provide the bait with which to ensnare Bonnie and Clyde, rather than Hamer locating them purely by logic and detection.

Methvin, knowing that he faced execution for his role in many of the gang's murders, eagerly agreed to help Hamer. He then lured

Bonnie and Clyde to his parent's home, on the pretext that he needed a lift, thereby creating the trap the police had been waiting for.

Henry Methvin did not profit from his involvement in the deaths of Bonnie and Clyde. Methvin killed a further policeman, officer Campbell, soon after his deal with Sheriff Hamer, and was lucky to escape the electric chair for this murder. Instead, he was imprisoned until 1949.

However, the justice which was enacted upon Henry Methvin because of his betrayal of Bonnie and Clyde was infinitely crueler than that exacted on him by the courts of Oklahoma for his other murders.

In April, not long after his release from prison, Methvin was knocked unconscious whilst walking home. He was then taken to a railway line in Louisiana, and secured to the track. Who Methvin's assailant was is still a mystery to this day.

When Henry Methvin was found by the authorities, he had been killed by a passing train, which had severed his body in two.

Intriguingly, the youngest member of the police posse, Ted Hinton, suggested another version of events in his post-humous autobiography *Ambush*. Here, Hinton claimed that it was Ivy, and not Henry Methvin who had been bullied by Sheriff Hamer into ensnaring Bonnie and Clyde.

Ivy Methvin, whose real name was Ivan, was Henry's father. Allegedly, Ivy was told by officers Henderson Jordan and Sheriff Hamer that Henry would be executed unless Ivy cooperated with the authorities. This included gaining information which would result in a successful ambush, regardless of the risks involved to Ivy or his family.

Indeed, in some versions of events, it has been suggested that Ivy was tied to one of the trees alongside the Louisiana road to make sure that he complied with the police. Ivy's truck was then parked in such a way that Bonnie and Clyde would slow or even stop to investigate what had happened.

Ivy Methvin was found dead just sixteen months before his son was killed in 1949. He had also been killed by a train on a railroad track. It has never been confirmed whether this was another revenge killing for the deaths of Bonnie and Clyde.

In *Ambush,* Hinton said that the members of the police posse had agreed not to tell the truth about the police blackmail until all six of them had died. This pact meant that the officers involved could avoid any of the potential public scandal. There could easily have been a Media uproar if police officers admitted to having unethically forced an innocent civilian into a highly dangerous situation, which could easily have resulted in their death. Hamer and his group had also lied about their methods and the success of their techniques and procedures. But by choosing to conceal what happened until *Ambush* was posthumously published, it is now impossible to question either Hinton or the other five officers and thereby ascertain the truth.

To further damage the reputation of these six officers, their behavior and motivations have since been questioned.

In part, this is a result of the uncertainty about what happened immediately before the shooting began. In the official version, the police posse called for Bonnie and Clyde to surrender, and only began shooting when there was no other option. However, the uncertainty about which officer called out to the pair makes this story seem suspicious. It is strange that there were no consistent statements between the six police officers who were present when this must have been a key moment that they would remember. It is more likely that none of the officers issued a warning, but instead immediately opened fire.

Moreover, in Hinton and Alcorn's account, the police fired at Bonnie and Clyde's car whilst it was still moving. It is likely that there was no cautionary shout before shots were fired. This would confirm the suggestion that Lee Simmons himself wanted Bonnie and Clyde shot dead, rather than risk losing them whilst they were being apprehended.

Many historians today have accused, particularly officers Hamer and Jordan, of being more interested in fame and financial rewards than they ever were in the law or justice.

For instance, it has been alleged that Sheriff Hamer was disgusted with the one hundred and eighty dollars which he was offered per month as a salary for his work. He had to be tempted by a promise from Lee Simmons that if Hamer apprehended Bonnie and Clyde, he could help himself to any of their assets. Simmons didn't care what happened to recovered objects, he simply wanted Bonnie and Clyde. Hamer was also happy to make a profit from the criminal pair.

Simmons' alleged promise would become important immediately after Bonnie and Clyde were killed.

Not only did Ted Hinton accuse him of being behind the blackmail of Ivy Methvin, but Officer Henderson Jordan, one of the Louisiana police officers, also caused anger in many circles when he attempted to keep the car in which Bonnie and Clyde had been murdered.

The Ford V8 had been stolen from a lady called Ruth Warren and should have been returned to her. However, Jordan felt entitled to keep the car, on the basis that he felt that he, and the other five police officers, had earned it through their actions. In the end, it took a court order to force Jordan to give the car back to Ruth Warren.

Once Ruth Warren had her car returned, complete with extensive gunshot damage and blood stains, she rented and eventually sold the car. In the hands of new owner, Charles Stanley, the Ford V8, which became known as "the death-car", was a popular crowd-puller at various fairs and shows across America.

The Ford V8 where Bonnie and Clyde died is currently on display at the Whiskey Pete's casino and hotel near Las Vegas in California. It is now a tourist attraction alongside the complex's four restaurants, swimming pool, and shops. The car sits in the entrance lobby, in front of a painting which depicts Bonnie and Clyde being ambushed and fired upon by police.

Bonnie and Clyde were likely killed without warning, by officers who were determined to execute them, using whatever means necessary. We may never know what happened on that Louisiana road, but the evidence that has since emerged about police and public behavior is both deeply shocking and brutal. This naturally changes how we may interpret the behavior and actions of Bonnie and Clyde themselves.

Bonnie and Clyde: The Aftermath

Bonnie and Clyde have refused to die; at least as far as popular culture is concerned. Ever since they were shot by police in 1934, stories about Bonnie and Clyde have been told in books, films, and musicals. The pair have proved enduringly popular, and their exploits continue to be reimagined and retold to the present day.

One of the most famous films was the 1967 *Bonnie and Clyde* directed by Arthur Penn. This film was crucial in turning many of the gang's exploits into tales focused on Bonnie Parker and Clyde Barrow. The film was initially supported by Blanche Barrow, who was one of the few surviving gang members, but she grew to hate her representation by the time the film was finally made.

Bonnie and Clyde was also enjoyed by many young people. Indeed, the film made the real-life Bonnie and Clyde into symbols of the desires of many young people to attack the social taboos and social constraints of the time.

A Broadway musical, which enjoyed over sixty-nine performances, was the 2009 musical, titled *Bonnie and Clyde.* Although it failed to convince the theatre critics, the musical was nominated for several awards. It featured songs such as "This world will remember me", "dyin' aint so bad", and "raise a little hell".

Conclusion

Given that autobiographies such as police officer Hinton's *Ambush* created more uncertainties than it resolved, it is likely that we will never really know who Bonnie Parker and Clyde Barrow were, or exactly what they did during their brief lives. But whether they were vicious murderers, loveable outlaws, or a combination of the two, they have been immortalized within American history and popular culture. As Clyde's epitaph accurately summarizes, Bonnie and Clyde may be dead, but they have not been forgotten.

Printed in Great Britain
by Amazon